Creative Crafts

Christmas Crafts

Hilary Devonshire, John Lancaster, Lyndie Wright

Consultant: Henry Pluckrose

Photography: Chris Fairclough

FRANKLIN WATTS
LONDON • SYDNEY

This edition 2004

Franklin Watts
96 Leonard Street
London EC2A 4XD

Franklin Watts Australia
45-51 Huntley Street,
Alexandria, NSW 2015

Hardback edition published
under the series title Fresh Start.

Editor: Jenny Wood
Design: K & Co

ISBN 0 7496 5896 7

Printed in Belgium

Contents

This book describes activities which use the following:

Beads
Blu-Tack
Brushes for glue and paint
Candles
Card (thick and thin; manilla, white and coloured)
Christmas cards (old)
Compass (for drawing circles)
Cotton or nylon thread
Cotton wool
Craft knife
Crayons
Cutting board
Dowel rods
Embroidery thread
Fabric scraps (ribbon, lace, felt, calico)
Felt-tip pens (black and coloured, waterproof and water-soluble)
Garden canes
Glue (wall-paper paste, PVA, Bostik)
Jars (old, for water and paste)
Household knife (old)
Magazines
Metallic ink marker pens (gold and silver)
Modelling clay
Needle
Newspapers

Paints — water-based
— poster
— tempera
— acrylic
Paper — cartridge paper
— foil paper
— sugar or construction paper
— typing paper
(all in a range of colours)
Paper punch (for making holes)
Pencils (lead and coloured)
Ping-pong balls
Plaster of Paris
Plastic food containers (e.g. yoghurt pots) in a range of sizes
Printing pads (made from sponge)
Rags (old cloths for cleaning)
Ruler (metal, and plastic or wooden)
Saucer or old plate for mixing paints
Saw
Scissors
Shoe boxes (old)
Silver foil
Sticky tape
String (or nylon fishing line)
Sweet wrappings
Twigs
Water
Wool (lengths of 2 or 3 ply)

'Against the feast of Christmas every man's house, also their parish churches were decked with ivy, holly and whatever the season offered to be green. Even the streets were likewise garnished.'

This account of Christmas decorations was written over 400 years ago, and the activities which are included in this book have strong links with our historical past. Boys and girls have made decorations, gifts and cards for many centuries. And of course, in celebrating Christmas, we are also celebrating the story of Mary and Joseph and the Christ child born in a stable in Bethlehem almost 2,000 years ago.

Not all our Christmas customs have such a long history. Prince Albert (Queen Victoria's husband) is thought to have introduced the Christmas tree to England in 1841 when he ordered a fir tree to be taken to Windsor Castle and decorated with candles. The fir tree *'ablaze with lighted candles'* was the traditional way in which many people on the mainland of Europe celebrated Christmas. Prince Albert, a German, thought that his children should enjoy the beauty of the tree and experience the excitement of opening the presents which lay beneath it.

The sending of Christmas cards also dates from Victorian times. The custom became very popular in Britain, probably because of the introduction of a postal service (by Roland Hill in 1840) which meant that, for the first time, letters and cards could be sent very cheaply to any address in the British Isles.

I hope you enjoy using this book and that you will have fun making the Christmas Crafts.

The merry time of Christmas
Is drawing very near,
I wish you a happy Christmas
And a happy New Year,
A pocket full of money
A cellar of good cheer
And a fat pig to last you
Till next Christmas be here.

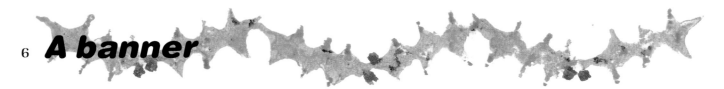

A banner

A paper scroll, or banner, is quite simple to design and make. When completed it can be hung from a rafter or small hook in the ceiling so that it swings gently, or suspended flat against a wall. Either way it should be an effective Christmas decoration.

You may, of course, decide to make two or three scrolls with different messages or designs. If you do decide to make a number of scrolls, then vary their sizes and colours.

You will need a pencil, a ruler, scissors, paper (black, white or coloured), PVA glue, a glue brush, a dowel rod (thin sticks or tightly rolled newspaper are useful substitutes), a saw, water-based paints, a paintbrush, a metallic ink marker pen (gold or silver), thin string or nylon fishing line and coloured felt-tip pens.

1 Measure then cut out a long, thin rectangle of paper approximately 4cm longer than you wish the finished scroll to be. The example shown here is 10cm x 14.7cm. Paint a strip of glue across each end of the paper.

2 Cut two lengths of dowel rod with the saw. Each one should be 4cm longer than the width of the scroll. Colour these with brightly coloured paint or with your metallic marker pen. Place one at each end of the paper, above or below the strip of glue, as appropriate.

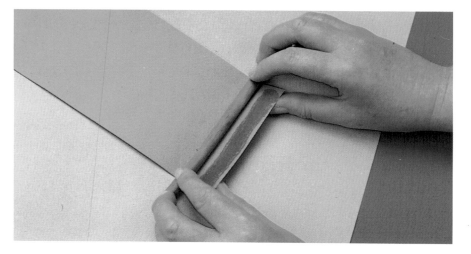

3 Roll the glued strips over on to the dowel rods, making a loop at each end of the scroll.

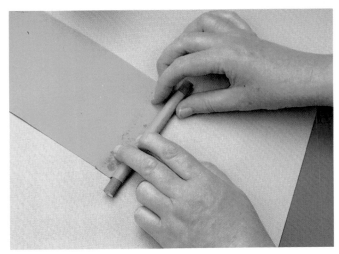

4 Make sure the loops are securely fixed. Tie the ends of a length of string around the ends of the top piece of dowel then knot into a single strand. This will enable you to hang up the scroll.

5 Try decorating your scroll by painting a border all the way around the edges. Use strong, bold lines. Add a snow scene in the centre or simply paint a colourful pattern of squares, circles or curving lines.

6 Draw MERRY CHRISTMAS in decorated letters down the length of one side of the scroll...

7 ...and HAPPY NEW YEAR on the other side!

If you want to make a very long scroll which could hang in a stairwell or in a high room, then you will need to attach one or more sheets of paper together. Using different colours of paper will make this look very effective.

A Christmas pyramid

This decorated pyramid is a hanging decoration. Several pyramids dangling from a small hoop can look very attractive.

You will need white card, a pencil, a ruler, scissors, crayons, sticky tape, cotton thread or thin string, PVA glue and a glue brush.

1 On white card and using an equilateral triangle as a template, draw a group of four triangles. They should be positioned exactly as shown in the photograph. Draw a tab along one side of each of the three outside triangles, as shown, then carefully cut out the whole shape. When folded, this will make a pyramid.

2 Draw a picture or pattern on each triangle. This design shows the Three Wise Men and the Star of Bethlehem.

3 Fold the shape along the sides of the centre triangle and along the tabs.

4 Using sticky tape, attach a thread to the inside of the pyramid at the top corner of one triangle.

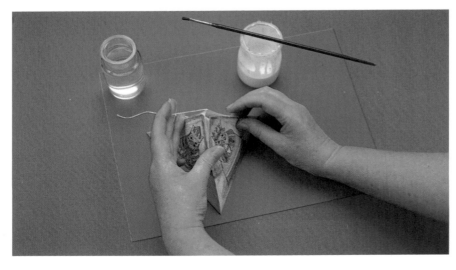

5 Glue each tab and stick the sides of the pyramid together. Hold the edges for a short time while the glue dries.

6 The finished pyramid. What other Christmas designs can you think of?

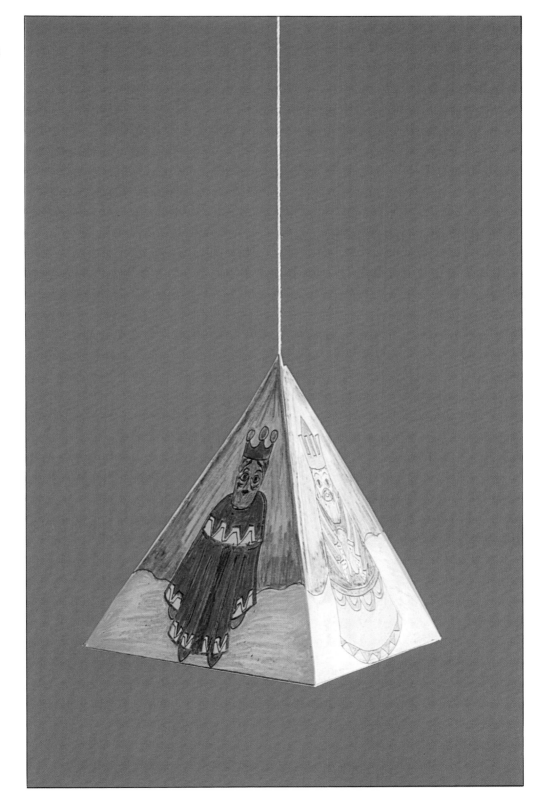

A mobile

When we put up paper streamers and other indoor Christmas decorations, we sometimes ignore the windows. Here is an idea for a window decoration.

You will need black or dark-coloured paper or thin card, scissors, white poster paint, a paintbrush, a needle, thin cotton or nylon thread, a garden cane and thin string or nylon fishing line.

1 Cut a large number of diamond shapes out of the paper or card. Vary the sizes, from about 4cm square to 10cm square. (The more shapes you produce, the more patterns you will have and the more effective your hanging will become.)

2 Paint a white pattern on both sides of each diamond shape. Vary these patterns, making some of them very simple and delicate, others bolder and more complicated.

3 Using the needle, make a small hole in the top corner of each diamond shape. Cut a length of thread for each shape. Vary the lengths of these threads so that the shapes will hang at different positions. Tie one end of a length of thread through each of the holes.

4 Attach a length of string to each end of the garden cane, and knot into a single strand. Hang the diamond shapes from the cane, then hang the complete cane from a small hook which should be very near to the top edge of a window.

The finished mobile should, if possible, fill the complete window space.

A 'pop-up' Christmas Card

This idea has a surprise Christmas message hidden inside the card!

You will need thin white and coloured card, felt-tip pens, scissors, a craft knife, a metal ruler and a small piece of ribbon.

1 Draw a Christmas stocking on a piece of coloured card 9cm x 11cm.

2 Cut out the stocking. Use the craft knife and ruler to make a slit 5cm long near the top.

3 On a piece of white card, draw and colour the head and shoulders of a clown. (Your drawing should be about 5cm wide and 8cm high). You will also need a strip of coloured card (a different colour from the stocking) 5cm wide and 15cm long.

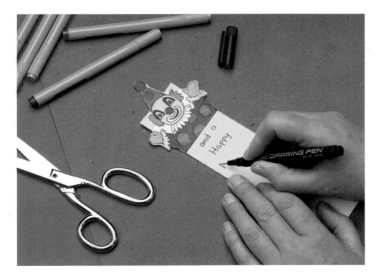

4 Cut out the clown and stick it to the top of the strip of card. Write a secret message underneath.

5 Push the strip of card down through the slit in the Christmas stocking so that the secret message is hidden. Write a message for the front of the Christmas card too, if you like.

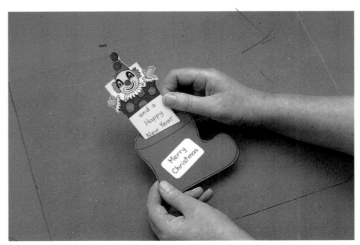

6 Fix a short piece of ribbon between the card strip and the stocking so that your Christmas card will stand up.

7 Your friends will be surprised when they push up the strip and read the secret message! Why not try some other 'pop-up' Christmas card designs?

The front of this Christmas card design is based on the word 'NOEL', although you might like to use the word 'XMAS' instead. It is a 'surprise' card for it has three flaps which, when lifted up, reveal hidden pictures.

You will need thin card or strong paper (any colour), a metal ruler, black and coloured felt-tip pens or water-based paints, scissors, a craft knife, a cutting board, one or two old Christmas cards, PVA glue and a glue brush.

1 (Left) Measure the shape of your Christmas card (18cm x 26cm) and cut it out. Fold the card in half. Using a black felt-tip pen, draw a rectangle (16cm x 11cm) on the front face of the folded card so that it has equal borders all around it. Divide this rectangle into four smaller, equal rectangles, then draw a horizontal centre line through the two centre rectangles.

2 (Left) Draw a large, bold letter 'N' in the left-hand rectangle. In two of the centre rectangles draw the letters 'O' and 'E'. Then draw a large letter 'L' to fill the right-hand rectangle. This completes the word 'NOEL'.

3 (Above) With brightly coloured felt-tip pens or paints colour the letters and background spaces of the Christmas card design.

Making the three flaps

The next step is to make the three surprise flaps. In the example, these are positioned below the letter 'O', above the letter 'E' and in the space formed to the right of the upward stroke of the letter 'L'.

4 Place the card on the cutting board. Cut along the sides and bottom edges of these three spaces using the craft knife and metal ruler.

5 Bend the flaps upwards. Decorate the spaces beneath the flaps with small pictures of snowmen, Father Christmas, candles, trees, holly and other pictures cut from old Christmas cards.

6 Cut another piece of card or paper 18cm x 13cm and glue this beneath the design. Remember to leave the flaps unglued.

7 The finished card.

8 Add a simple Christmas verse or message to the inside of the card. Either write your own, or cut out the verses from old cards and paste one inside each card you make.

A snowflake design

Snowflakes consist of small, usually hexagonal crystals. Here, hexagon shapes are made into a variety of snowflake patterns.

You will need thin white and coloured card, a pair of compasses, a pencil, a ruler, glue and a glue brush.

1 Draw a circle, radius 4.5cm, on a piece of white card. Mark a point on the edge of the circle.

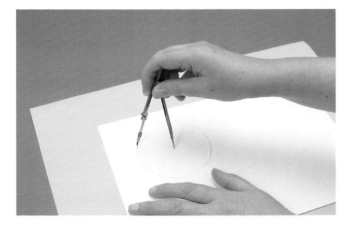

2 Keeping the compasses open at the same distance (4.5cm) and starting at the point you have made on the circle, mark another point further round the edge. Move round the circle in this way until you have six points around the edge.

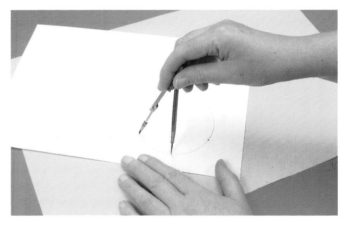

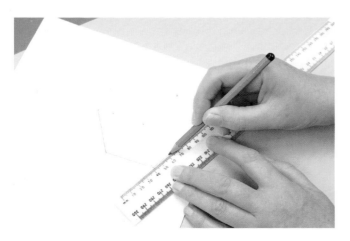

3 Using the pencil and ruler, join the points to make a hexagon.

4 Cut out your card hexagon, and use it as a template to draw a number of hexagons on white and coloured card.

5 Fold each hexagon in half. Now fold over one corner then the opposite corner to make a small triangle shape.

6 Cut out small pieces from the edges of each folded triangle. This is easier if you use thin card.

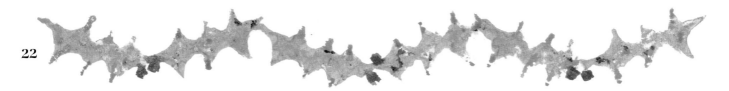

7 It's great fun unfolding your hexagons and discovering what patterns you have made. Every snowflake is different. Here are some red and white snowflake designs.

8 (Right) You can use your snowflake designs for Christmas cards. Here a red snowflake pattern is being stuck on to a white hexagon then on to a red card.

9 A selection of snowflake cards. On the left a 'see-through' design has been made by sticking a snowflake on to a cut-out hexagonal hole in the card.

The measurements given on the diagram below can be used to help you make envelopes for your Christmas cards. Remember that you can use coloured paper.

Envelopes don't have to be white, although the Post Office do prefer light colours as the names and addresses are easier to read.

1 The shape of the envelope before gluing.

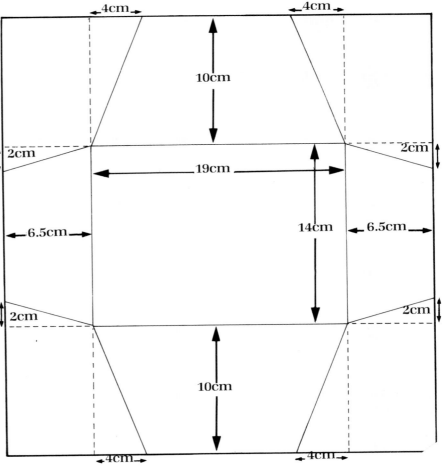

4cm   4cm

10cm

2cm   2cm

19cm

6.5cm   14cm   6.5cm

2cm   2cm

10cm

4cm   4cm

Crib in a shoe box

You will need an old shoe box, a
pencil, a ruler, thin white card,
poster or tempera paints or
crayons, a paintbrush, scissors,
PVA glue and a glue brush.

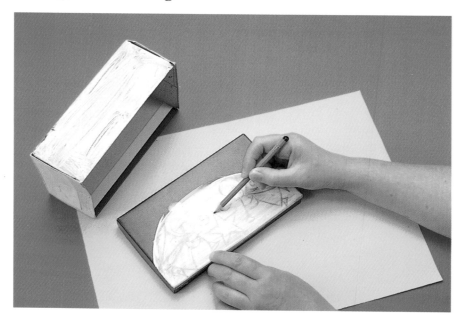

1 The shoe box set on its side
will be the stable, and the lid
can be used as a sky scene of
stars and angels. Start by
drawing the stars and angels in
the sky.

2 Draw the nativity figures on a
strip of white card. Measure
the box to make sure the
figures will fit inside. Leave a
blank area about 2cm deep
below each figure. This will be
folded over and stuck on to the
box.

3 Paint or colour the figures. Paint the sky scene too, and decorate the inside of the shoe box as a stable (a simple brown wash and a window are quite effective – see photograph **4**).

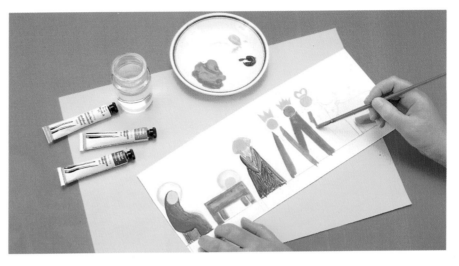

4 Cut out the painted sky and the figures. Be sure to leave the 2cm strip at the bottom of each one.

5 Bend back the strip on the base of each figure and glue it to the box base. Glue the sky scene to the top of the box.

6 The finished crib.

You can decorate your Christmas table with small standing figures such as a snowman or Father Christmas.

You will need white card, a pencil, a pair of compasses, a ruler, scissors, felt-tip pens, glue and a glue brush.

1 On a piece of card draw a small circle with a radius of 2cm for the head. Using the same centre point, draw a larger semi-circle (hold the ruler in position to give you the base line). This will be the body. Cut out the complete shape.

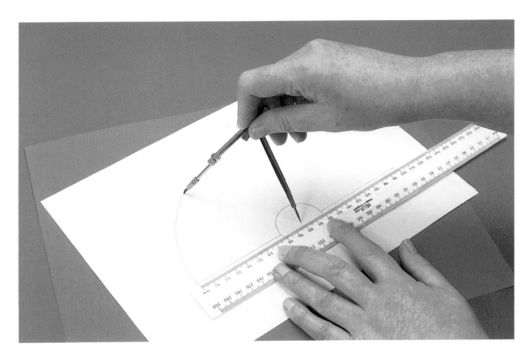

2 Use the card outline as a template. Draw round the shape on another piece of white card and add a face and hat as well as arms and hands. Colour your figure with felt-tip pens. This snowman has a red and green walking stick and blue eyes.

3 Cut out your figure. Cut carefully along the sides of the face and down the arms to the elbows.

4 Fold the body into a cone shape and glue the edges together at the back of the figure.

5 The finished figures. The Father Christmas in the centre has been made from red foil paper and decorated with cotton wool.

Christmas fairy

You will need three sheets of paper (each one a different colour), a pair of compasses, a pencil, scissors, felt-tip pens or silver and gold metallic ink marker pens, Bostik, a ping-pong ball and a craft knife.

1 Take one sheet of paper and, using the compasses, draw a circle 12cm in radius. Cut round the circle and cut a line from the edge to the centre. You will know where the centre is by the hole made by the compass point.

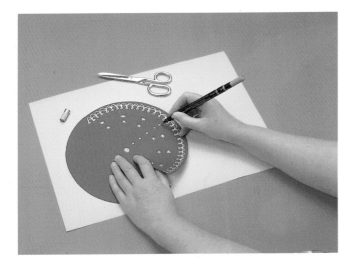

2 Carefully cut a small hole about 1cm across at the centre of the circle. Draw a pattern on half of the circle, using the felt-tip or metallic marker pens. This will be the fairy's skirt.

3 Carefully bend the circle to form a cone about 9cm across at the base. Glue the edges together. Make sure the skirt pattern is on the outside!

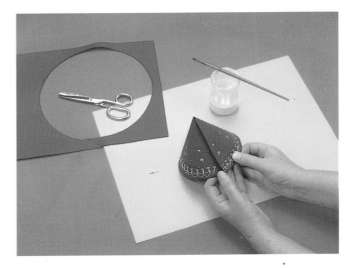

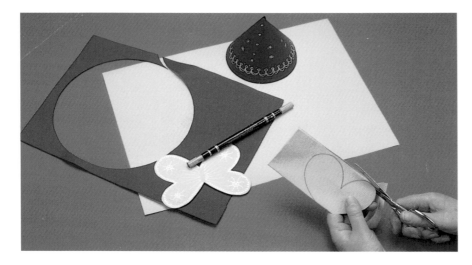

4 Take another sheet of paper (a different colour this time) and fold it in half. Draw and cut out a pair of wings, then decorate them with the felt-tip or metallic marker pens.

5 Take the ping-pong ball and cut a small hole (about 1cm across) with the craft knife. (You may need an adult to help with this.) Put a little Bostik around the edge of the hole and stick the ball on to the cone.

6 Glue the wings in position, too.

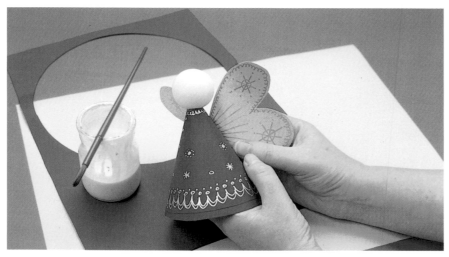

7 Fold a scrap of paper the same colour as the skirt and cut out a simple pair of arms. Decorate these and glue them on to the cone.

8 Cut out a star for the fairy to hold and glue it in position. Draw a face on the ping-pong-ball.

9 To make the hair, take a small piece of paper (a third colour, if possible). Cut strips at both ends and leave an uncut bit in the centre. If you would like your fairy to have curly hair, roll the strips around the end of the pencil.

10 Your fairy is now complete and ready for the Christmas tree!

Plaster candle holders

Cover yourself with an apron and your table or work surface with old newspapers before you try out this idea!

You will need Plaster of Paris ('finishing' or dental plaster is best), plastic containers to use as moulds, an old plastic container for mixing the plaster, candles, Blu-Tack, water, an old household knife, a piece of cloth, poster or acrylic paint and a paintbrush.

1 A collection of different-shaped containers which you can use as candle-holder moulds.

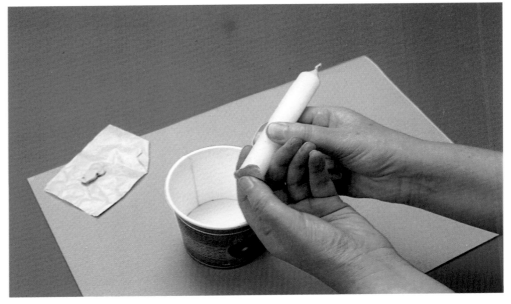

2 Select a mould and fasten a candle to it. Use Blu-Tack to hold the candle firmly in position. You don't want it falling over when you pour the plaster around it!

3 Pour into your mixing container as much water as would fill your mould. Slowly and evenly sprinkle Plaster of Paris into the water. Start at the outer edges of the mixing container and work towards the centre. Go on adding plaster until you are left with a dry island of plaster in the centre. Don't *mix* the plaster yet.

4 Now, working quickly, mix the plaster with your hands. Make sure it is lump-free!

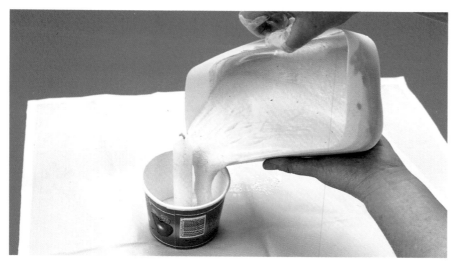

5 When it reaches a creamy consistency it is about to set, so pour it into the mould at once. Now wash and dry your hands. Be careful not to get plaster down the drain as it could cause a blockage.

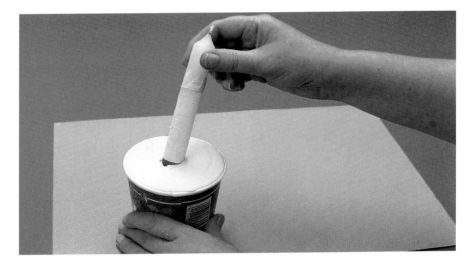

6 When the plaster is no longer runny, carefully remove the candle from the mould.

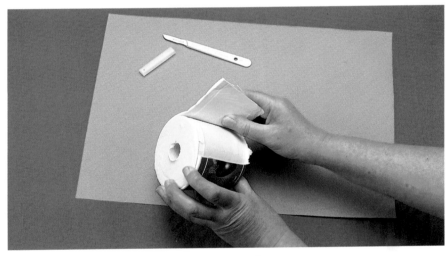

7 Wait about ten minutes, then take the plaster shape out of the mould. You may need to cut the mould to get the plaster out.

8 Using the old knife, cut patterns into the plaster shape. This is great fun to do, but take your time! It would be a pity to spoil your candle holder at this stage. Rub the crumbs of plaster off with an old cloth.

9 When dry, paint the carved shape with poster or acrylic paint.

10 A collection of candle holders, each one a different shape and design.

Some trees and bushes still have their leaves at Christmas, so you can use these to make a decorative centrepiece for your Christmas dinner table.

You will need a piece of card, modelling clay, silver foil, white paint, a paintbrush, some twigs (with leaves on), and small hanging decorations.

1 Shape some modelling clay on a piece of card as a base for the twigs.

2 Cover the modelling clay with silver foil. Paint the leaves and twigs with some white paint to look like snow. The ones shown here are from a laurel bush. Push the twigs into the modelling clay.

3 Make some small Christmas decorations to hang on the twigs. You can use some ideas from this book – for example, miniature figures (pp 27-28), pyramid (pp 9-11), and snowflakes (pp 20-22). You can even make a table mat for your decoration to stand on.

A Christmas print

You can make sponge prints of many Christmas shapes and patterns. Here a robin is used to make a Christmas picture.

You will need a thin sponge, a pen, scissors, card, PVA glue, a glue brush, paints, a paintbrush and white and coloured paper.

1 Draw a robin, or another shape of your choice, on the sponge and cut it out.

2 Glue the sponge robin on to the card. Leave to dry. Charge the sponge with paint, letting the paint soak in.

3 Make a print on white paper. Experiment to see how much paint you need to get a good print.

4 The finished design. The black paper background was textured by printing with a scrap of sponge and white paint. Holly leaves have been printed in a circle around the robin.

Bookmarks

Bookmarks are useful Christmas gifts for friends and relatives. They are attractive and easy to make.

You will need some stiff paper or card (white, black or coloured), a pencil, a ruler, scissors, a paper punch, coloured scrap paper (e.g. magazines, sweet wrappings, silver foil), PVA glue, a glue brush, felt-tip pens and coloured ribbon (thin) or string.

1 Draw a number of rectangles on the paper or card then cut them out carefully. A good size for each is 5cm x 25cm. Punch a small hole in the centre of each card near to the bottom edge.

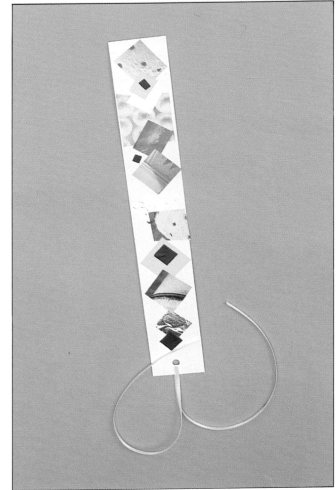

2 Cut a number of diamond shapes in varying sizes from the coloured scrap paper. Glue these diamonds on to the front of your bookmark. Make some of them overlap so that the design is more interesting.

3 Another idea is to draw a border around the edge of the bookmark with a black felt-tip pen. Fill in the space in the middle with circles, drawn freehand. These can overlap or touch, and you may vary them in size. Colour in your design.

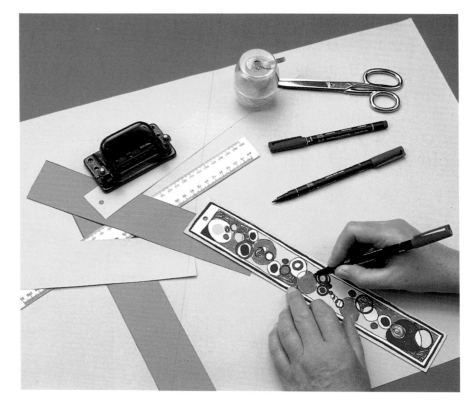

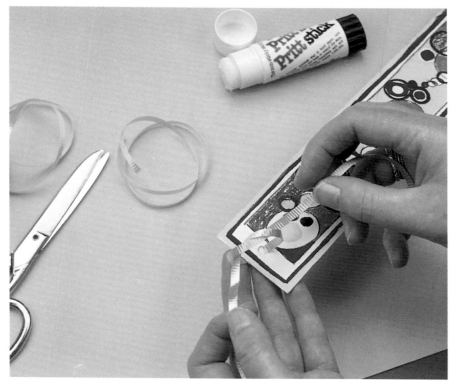

4 Complete the bookmark by adding a colourful tail. Take one or two lengths of coloured ribbon or string and pull them through the hole near the bottom edge of the bookmark. Put a touch of glue at the back to hold them in place.

5 The finished bookmark.

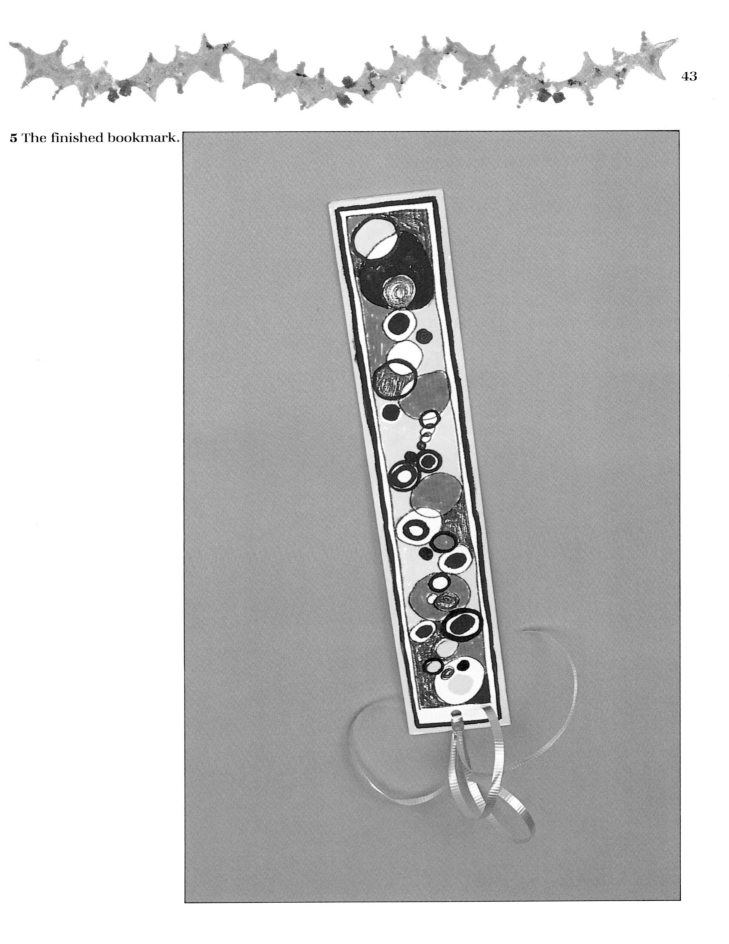

Finger puppets and stage

You will need calico, water-soluble felt pens, a paintbrush, scissors, a needle and thread, embroidery thread, wool, felt, beads, and bits of lace for decoration. For the stage you will need an old shoe box, a craft knife, a metal ruler, a pencil, tempera or poster paints and a paintbrush.

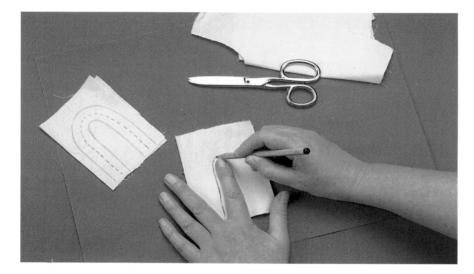

1 Place your finger on a folded piece of calico and draw round it. Draw a dotted line 1cm away. Draw a third line, a solid line, 1cm away from the dotted line. This third line you have drawn will be the cutting line. Cut out the finger puppet shape.

2 Sew along the dotted line using small running stitches. Finish off securely with a few stitches on top of each other. When you have done this, turn the shape inside out.

3 It may help to iron the calico shape before you start to colour it. Draw the puppet using water-soluble felt pens. These allow you to wash or fade the colours into each other. Experiment on a scrap of material first.

4 When the colour has dried, decorate the puppet with embroidery thread or wool for hair, a felt hat, bead eyes, a lace collar or whatever you choose. You can make as many finger puppets as you like.

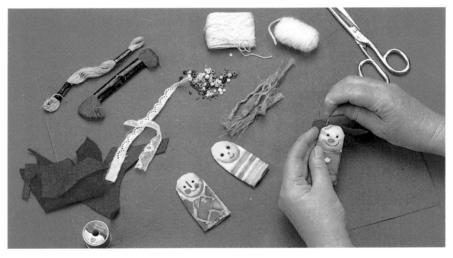

5 An old shoe box on end makes a very good stage for the finger puppets. Draw a rectangle in the bottom of the box. Using the craft knife and metal ruler, cut along three sides of this rectangle, leaving the upper side attached – this piece may be lifted up and used as a curtain.

6 Paint the box to look like a Punch and Judy booth. Your stage is ready for the puppets to give their show!

Most of the materials mentioned in this book are easy to obtain. Some are simply scrap materials and will cost you nothing. Others, such as paints, felt-tip pens, card and adhesives, can be purchased from stationers and/or artists' materials shops.

Materials in large quantities can be obtained through a school supplier such as NES ARNOLD, Findel House, Excelsior Road, Ashby Park, Ashby de la Zouch, Leicestershire LE65 1NG
0845 120 4525
www.nesarnold.co.uk

Paper
If you want to get a range of papers, both hand- and machine-made, you will find the following suppliers useful:
FRED ALDOUS LTD, 37 Lever Street, Manchester M1 1LW
www.fredaldous.co.uk
08707 517 300
ART EXPRESS, Design House, Sizers Court, Yeadon LS19 6DP
www.artexpress.co.uk
0800 731 4185
FALKINER FINE PAPERS LTD, 76 Southampton Row, London WC1B 4AR
020 7831 1151

TN LAWRENCE & SON LTD, 208 Portland Road, Hove, BN3 5QT
www.lawrence.co.uk
01273 260260
NES ARNOLD, as above.

For Australia, try looking at au.art-search.com and click on 'Art supply retailers'.

Brushes
Use white hog-hair brushes, which are hard-wearing and comparatively cheap. Sizes 6, 8 and 12 are recommended for the activities included in this book (size 6 for small-scale work, size 12 for large-scale work).

Wax crayons
Good quality wax crayons are made in a wide range of colours (including gold, silver and bronze) and thicknesses. They are obtainable from shops which sell artists' materials and from most stationers and department stores.